Business Habits For Increased Productivity And Sustained Success

The Art of Setting Goals In Business And Completing Them With Confidence

Business Habits For Increased Productivity And Sustained Success

Table of Contents

Introduction -..3

Chapter 1 – Being An Innovator......................................4

Chapter 2 – Setting S.M.A.R.T Goals...........................16

Chapter 3 – Procrastination And Motivation...............27

Chapter 4 – Organization & Prioritization...................39

Chapter 5 – Managing Your Team: Bonus Habits....43

Conclusion...47

Introduction

I want to thank you and congratulate you for purchasing the book *Business Habits for Increased Productivity and Sustained Success: The Art of Setting Goals in Business and completing them with Confidence.*

This book contains proven steps and strategies on maximizing productivity for your business and professional life.

In this book, you will find numerous, easy-to-follow 'Business Habits' that maximize the likelihood of your business' success, especially in the long run. Outlined in each chapter are fundamental lessons to help you achieve the greatest productivity and get real results!

Thanks again for purchasing this book. I hope you enjoy it!

Business Habits For Increased Productivity And Sustained Success

Chapter 1 – Being An Innovator

By the end of this Chapter, you will have learned all about:

- Realizing your business' limits
- Identifying your own aspirations and incorporating them in your business
- Creating a vision for your business that everyone can relate to
- Determining the things that can limit the potential of your business

If you want to learn about improving your productivity for your business or professional life, it is important to focus first on improving your character as a leader. For this chapter, your main objective is not to unlock your true potential but to *realize* what you have to offer in the business world. The difference is that your potential has been there all along, you simply need to realize it and believe in it.

What is the Potential of Your Business?

It is innate for every person to dream of something better for the future. It is the core quality that made mankind – and all the organizations formed within it – into the civilization it is now. This instinctive desire for better things in life is what pushed us to achieve more. This is why *aspiring* is considered the first step to being successful, but there is only so much a single person can do before he requires the participation of a devoted team for great success.

Since we were children, we were asked questions about our dreams and aspirations. Your family has expected a lot from you from the very beginning. In turn, you have aspired to great things for your future in order to prove yourself. It is a gift that most people have as children. Chances are, you never even thought about being successful in business when you were young.

Times are changing. In the past, people depended on job security and monthly paychecks to survive, but this is not the case anymore. If you observe modern society, tax laws are felt more by the working people, and wages are no longer enough to get by.

Starting out in life with a bag full of dreams is not the only gift you have as a person. You should know that every part of you, from head to toe, is built to become an achiever that will ultimately accomplish great success. Yet, if you would look at it closer, this is the very desire that made you choose to run a business in the first place.

In short, everybody's true potential is nothing less than *great success.* Remember that every successful business in history started out with nothing more than what you have right now, some even started with less. Every aspiring businessman is born this way.

What really prevents great success in business?

The first thing you should know is the one thing that influences everything in your life and your business – your own *mindset.* This is because everything that can generate your success or lead to your failures can be found there.

As a child, your mind was probably filled with energy and optimism about your future, but as time goes by, you slowly fill yourself with doubt, especially after experiencing difficulties in life. These doubts ultimately limit your potential and your ability to accomplish goals and objectives. Furthermore, this negative mindset passes through to your team – affecting their productivity.

In realizing your own potential for success in business, you need to harness these old desires of yours and integrate them with your passion. Remember that loving what you do is one of the key ingredients for success in business. Do you have an idea for something never seen before? Do you consider yourself a pioneer in the industry you love?

As the first step in realizing your potential for the business you have chosen, you need to establish a long-term vision. What do you have to offer the industry that you would consider an *innovation?* Remember in the world of business, there are countless imitators, but there is a short supply of real innovators.

Being an innovator does not mean you should come up with a new piece of technology from the ground up. Sometimes, all a successful innovator needs to do is to create a new *way* to use an already existing technology. It should be a bold and daring attempt, not something that has been done before. Do you think successful businesses were remembered for their imitations? *No.* They are remembered for the wild ideas they believed in.

Every person in business is capable of coming up with such ideas. If you are in an industry you are passionate about, then you are more than capable of concocting your own innovation.

Focus on what you think the industry lacks, or what can improve the technology in an efficient and *profitable* way. It is important that you have the courage to believe in your own ideas. However, there are certain mindsets that can limit your potential in creating an innovation.

To be more specific, here are some of limiting mindsets:

1. **Fear of Failures –** This is the most common reason why a lot of people hesitate in taking

chances for creating innovations. It is no secret that everyone finds failures and mistakes undesirable, especially if a person focuses on the losses of each failure. Remember that most businesses in history were not built successfully on the first attempt.

2. **False Contentment** – A lot of people actually inhibit their own vision by being content with what they already have. Although this is not necessarily a bad thing, too much reliance on what is readily available will definitely eliminate your chance for something better. Ask yourself, are you comfortable being an *insignificant* player of the industry? Or do you want to take the first step toward creating a huge impact that will change the industry forever?

3. **Uncertainty** – Another mindset that can limit a person's innovative potential is uncertainty. It is true that no one is certain about the future of their business. In fact, each businessman can sometimes feel confused on what he really wants and whether or not he is in the *right* industry. If you really feel you have nothing to offer to make your business stand out – *leave*. Try someplace else you are comfortable studying and exploring for hours. Remember that as a businessman, it is your duty to know every piece of information in

your industry, which leads to the last mindset that inhibits a person's innovative ability:

4. **Ignorance** – Lastly, you can never ignore the importance of knowledge for success and productivity in business. It is true that everyone is born capable of great success, but this is wasted if you are not willing to learn and acquire useful knowledge. This is why it is important for you as a leader to be passionate about what your business does.

These four mindsets are the most common reasons a lot of people end up limiting their potential for innovation. There can also be other things in a person's mind that can lead to limiting his own potential for business success, but once you identify these four, the next step should become clear for you. By the time you are finished with this book, you will have all the answers needed for dealing with these.

Chapter Activity:

The first step in achieving great success in life is to rediscover your ability to aspire. You will use this to redefine the vision of your company – something that every member believes in.

Note: For all of the activities in this book, you will need to keep a *personal journal.* It can be written in a physical notebook or on a computer.

Visualization is actually the first step of effective goal setting (to be discussed next chapter). Basically, visualization can dictate what your business can achieve. If you have partners, it may be a good idea for you.

Step 1: Start with Point A

The first step of visualization is to consider the state of your business right now. This will be your starting position, or "Point A". In your personal journal, write down your assets, skills, experiences, and valuable contacts. There is no formal way of doing this. Just write them all down on one page, and make it as clear and concise as possible.

Step 2: Identify your Point B

The second step is most important. In this step, you will simply visualize your *ultimate goal.* Try to visualize goals you have had prior to beginning your business. As to not limit your potential in other industries, feel free to visualize goals unrelated to your current business (as long as you are willing to pursue them). Just make sure your Point B is as clear and specific as possible.

Also, make sure your Point B is outrageously *awesome.* There is no reason for you to settle for anything less. Just raise the bar as high as you can and never lose sight of the finish line.

Step 3: Redefine your Business' Vision

Finalize everything you want to have in your Point B and write it down in a single paragraph. Ideally, you need to ask the opinion of everyone in your organization about this paragraph. It is important that every single person in your company, no matter the position, believes in this single paragraph. From now on, declare this as your 'vision'. If your business already has an established vision, try to compare your purpose in Point B and *rewrite* it for the better.

Creating a motivation collage for yourself and your team

As an individual

After identifying these important details about your Point B, you can try creating your own *motivation collage* to maximize the effect. A motivation collage is a collection of pictures of the things you want to have in life. It can be the photo of your dream car, your dream house, or your dream vacation destination.

A motivation collage can be something big enough to be on your wall or small enough to be in your wallet. It is entirely up to you to decide the size of your motivation collage. You also do not necessarily need exact photographs of what you want. Something of close resemblance should suffice.

As a business

For smaller businesses, you can create a single motivation collage for every person in your team. Take note that your subordinates are just as crucial to success as you are. This means your motivation as a leader is useless if your team does not believe in it. With this in mind, you should all be motivated as a unit.

A motivation collage is used for gaining motivation whenever you or your team members need a boost. It gives your team a sense of direction, or something to shoot for. Remember, sometimes you need to paint the target yourself in order to hit the bull's-eye.

Business Habit #1: Guided Visualization

Throughout this book, you will find *Business Habits* leaders can use to increase productivity and maximize success in business. Business Habits will be introduced in a way that will suit the lessons presented in each chapter.

The habit of guided visualization is what a lot of people recognize simply as *daydreaming.* Others call it the *law of attraction.* However, it is important for you to guide your mind in attracting or daydreaming about the *right things*. In other words, you should always have a consistent visualization of everything in your Point B.

Important Note:

Business Habits For Increased Productivity And Sustained Success

If done individually, you can increase your self-motivation as well as your productivity as a leader, but remember you cannot maintain positive motivation if no one else in your organization feels it.

Once you have done this yourself, make sure every person in your business does it as well. In maximizing the productivity of your business, the workplace and the people in it must be positive.

Finding your own visualization

If you have done all the previous activities in this chapter, then it should be easy for you to have a consistent visualization every time. A motivation collage makes this process much easier.

Guided visualization works for all kinds of goals and objectives. Keep on visualizing, and think as if you have already accomplished these things. Believe it or not, you may be doing this habit for hours a day.

The best way to implement this Business Habit is to do it in the morning upon waking up or, oddly enough, while taking a shower. You should never substitute your productivity for a session of daydreaming. This means you should snap out of your visualizations during work and business meetings.

Doing this habit before sleeping is a bad idea though. While visualizations can be relaxing, they can keep you up at night when you should be resting to recover your energy.

Here are other benefits of the habit of guided visualization:

1. **Increased Creativity**
2. **Increased Memory**
3. **Empathy**
4. **Better Moods**

Lastly, remember that guided visualizations or daydreams will not get the job done but will certainly get you started on the right track. Read the next chapter to find out what comes next.

In Application

Motivating your team is one of your responsibilities as a leader. Guiding them to having a positive outlook through visualizations is proven to be an effective way of motivating.

For small businesses

Make it a rule for every person in your business to put at least one photograph in a single motivation collage. A good idea would be to use a bulletin board big enough to allow everyone's contribution.

Chapter 2 – Setting S.M.A.R.T Goals

By the end of this Chapter, you will have learned all about:

- *The definition of S.M.A.R.T goals*
- *How to create goals for business*
- *How to create short-term goals from long-term goals*

- *How to apply the S.M.A.R.T criteria to your personal life*
- *Seeing better results with your goals*

In the previous chapter, you learned about the Business Habit of guided visualization. It is, in fact, an activity you have probably already done a couple of times before. This chapter is all about acting on your visualizations (or *planning* to do so).

You may already know about the two main types of goals, which are the *short-term goals* and *long-term goals.* In the world of business, short-term generally means goals or business objectives that can be accomplished within 12 months. Anything that will take more than a year to be accomplished or felt will be considered long-term.

If you are running a business, you should already have a long-term goal in mind. Notice that this is probably closely related to your visualizations created in the previous chapter. It is also a good idea to set a span of time or *deadline* for your long-term goals. This is usually between 3-5 years.

Here are additional tips for creating your long-term goals:

1. **Create them yourself (or with your own team)** – To have more realistic long-term

goals, it must be yours to begin with. It must be something that you, as a business or as an individual, will find worthwhile.

2. **Create more of them** – The best thing about creating goals and visualizations is that they are free. For major long-term goals, it is ideal to create about 5-10 goals for your business, career, and personal life. These major goals should be of extreme importance.

Of course, it is imperative for you to identify short-term goals for your business as well. If you remember the activity in the previous chapter, this part is all about moving from Point A to Point B. In other words, your enterprise will focus on the closing the gap between these two points.

In time, you will have to write down these goals and make them visible to other people in your business, but first, here are proven strategies for effective goal setting, beginning with the use of S.M.A.R.T:

The S.M.A.R.T Criteria

The S.M.A.R.T criteria have always been used as a guide for setting objectives in business management. With a few tweaks, it can also be applied to a person's individual life.

S.M.A.R.T stands for *Specific, Measurable, Achievable, Realistic,* and *Time-bound.* The criteria describe the quality of an effective goal or objective.

Business Habits For Increased Productivity And Sustained Success

Here is a brief overview of each element of the S.M.A.R.T criteria:

1. **Specific** – A goal must target a specific outcome or end result. The details must be complete and very clear. The easiest way to be specific when it comes to your goals is to identify the following:

    a. *What exactly should be accomplished?*

    b. *Who are the people involved?*

    c. *Where will this objective/goal be accomplished?*

    d. *What are the requirements or existing obstacles?*

    e. *Why will this objective or goal benefit the business?*

2. **Measurable** – Creating measurable goals is an important aspect of effective goal setting. This focuses on the importance of measuring the progress of the completion of a specific goal. It also eases the management process by answering the questions:

    a. *How much/many is needed?*

    b. *How far is the goal from being attained?*

    c. *What are the necessary adjustments that need to be made?*

d. *How effective is a particular strategy as opposed to another?*

3. **Achievable** – Previously, you were given the idea that you should create the best possible goals for yourself or your business, but it is also important for you to not go overboard and set goals that are unrealistic. If there are certain things that are out of your control (certain laws, current technology, etc.), then maybe you should focus on something less ambitious. Note that this can also mean *Assignable* in the S.M.A.R.T criteria. This simply means that each responsibility involved with the accomplishment of a particular goal can be distributed amongst your team. This is effective in creating smaller objectives and short-term goals.

4. **Relevant** – Effective goals must always have a discernable impact on the business. This impact must be observable by everyone in the business. Make sure the resources you invest in a particular goal or objective is worth it in the end.

5. **Time-bound** – The last part of the S.M.A.R.T criteria stresses the significance of establishing urgency in all goals and objectives. In setting goals effectively, it is required for you to establish a deadline that gives your team the

much-needed *push.* Time-bound goals also make them much easier to measure.

Creating Short-term Goals

If you currently run a business, then you probably already have an established set of short-term goals. If not, then you are either just starting out or already failing. Either way, here are quick tips on how to create short-term goals:

1. **Measure its Impact** – Even though short-term goals can occur in months, weeks, or even within this very day, it must have a measureable contribution toward a long-term goal. When creating short-term goals, it is always good to start with a major long-term goal and begin creating smaller objectives or *milestones.*

2. **Create even Smaller Objectives** – Even short-term goals themselves can be further divided into smaller parts. Of course, these parts will make the entire enterprise a lot easier and manageable. Take note that these smaller objectives can still be broken down into smaller objectives.

3. **Create a Timetable** – A timetable is basically a breakdown of your objectives in a week's time. There is no efficient way of including long-term goals in your timetable, but it is

perfect for organizing your short-term goals and objectives, as well as managing and distributing your time for all your tasks and responsibilities. You will find a complete guide on creating a timetable at the end of this chapter.

4. **Create Accountability** – An important aspect of goal setting, short-term or not, is to tell someone else involved. This is to establish accountability and improve your sense of responsibility for the objective, especially for business objectives that concern every member of your team.

Business Habit #2: Creating Checklists

A prominent quality of an achiever is the ability to constantly create objectives. No matter what you are doing, be it for business or for your personal life, it should be set as an objective *formally.* A simple habit that improves productivity and success is to have an everyday checklist of tasks and other responsibilities.

A checklist can be written on anything, preferably on something compact and easy to carry. Other than incorporating your timetable with your checklist, there is no special rule in creating them. The *priority* of your daily objectives should also be considered when creating checklists. Prioritization of objectives and goals for both long-term and short-term will be discussed in the next chapter.

For now, you can begin creating your checklist of daily tasks and activities for *tomorrow*.

Chapter Activity:

Creating a checklist is ideally done before starting your day at the office or in your place of business. Of course, you are free to create empty spaces on your checklist to make room for any additional task.

For this chapter's activity, you will create a quick and easy checklist for your tasks on the following day. Make sure to plan your objectives using the S.M.A.R.T criteria. In order to be more efficient with your time, it is important to make this process as organized and clear as possible. Here is how:

Step 1: Create a Timetable

It is much better to create your weekly timetable before you begin creating your checklist. Your timetable and checklist should be two separate documents. While your checklist is often updated and temporary, your timetable should be permanent *but* flexible.

In being flexible, your timetable should contain *empty slots* for checklist objectives. These empty slots are basically hours of the day when you are not engaged in other, equally important, activities.

In determining these empty slots, you first need to identify your weekly routines. These routines are the activities you cannot avoid. Here are examples of routine activities:

- *Driving*
- *Sleeping*
- *Meals*
- *Work hours*

You need to fill your entire table with these activities first. After doing this, you should be able to determine your free hours, which will be considered the *empty slots* in your timetable.

The length of each empty slot in your timetable can be for 30 minutes up to 1 hour each. This will make the activities in your timetable a lot easier to manage. Move on to the next step before you write down activities and tasks into your timetable.

Step 2: Assess your Objectives

Of course, you will need to identify your short-term objectives first. As you identify your short-term objectives, make sure you use the S.M.A.R.T criteria to set them effectively. Use the following questions to make sure each objective is S.M.A.R.T-ready.

1. *Specific* – What exactly should this objective be accomplishing?

2. *Measurable* – What are the indicators and resources you should watch out for?

3. *Assignable* – Who will be the people involved with the accomplishment of this objective? (Make sure they are fully aware of the tasks and responsibilities.)

4. *Relevant* – What other parts of your business will benefit from this objective? What is its impact?

5. *Time-bound* – How long will this objective take to be completed? (Take note that objectives can last for a few hours up to several weeks.)

Step 3: Write the Checklist

After making sure every objective you come up with fits the S.M.A.R.T criteria, you must then write them down using the *3 T's – Task name, Team,* and *Time.*

For example, if your objective is to order and acquire 100 units of Product X within the week, this is what the checklist objective should look like:

Task Name	**Team**
Time	
Order Product X	Merchandising
7 days	

Feel free to list as many objectives as you can. Take a look at your previous responsibilities, including any issues in your business that need attention. If you are running a business with a particularly large staff, it may be a good idea to call a meeting with your subordinates to find such issues.

Creating your checklist should not take much space, meaning it can easily be written in a small section of your personal journal. You can also use simple writing software such as *Notepad* or *Sticky Notes* to create quick checklists. Other than these, there are other productivity tools that will be discussed later on in this book.

Remember to keep your checklist as simple as possible. After looking at the particular objective listed above, you should then allot the appropriate amount of time for all responsibilities involved with said objective. This leads to the last step of this activity:

Step 4: Fill your timetable

Unlike your checklist, it is better for your timetable to be located in a place where everyone can see it. It can be posted on a bulletin board, written on a whiteboard, or accessed in your business network.

If you want, you can also create a more private timetable that contains your planned objectives and other activities for your personal life. Remember that your productivity outside of your place of work is just as important for success.

Finally, never forget to update your checklist as often as possible. Actively add more tasks while *checking off* completed ones. Doing these simple things will give you a sense of accomplishment needed to motivate you to achieve more.

Chapter 3 – Procrastination And Motivation

By the end of this Chapter, you will have learned all about:

- *Simple techniques to prevent procrastination in your workplace*
- *Ways to lessen procrastination in your team*
- *Motivate your team to complete more tasks*
- *Activities you can enjoy and be productive with at the same time*
- *How to build and maintain productivity for the long run*

Procrastination can be described as the direct opposite of productivity. By word, it is defined as the practice of doing insignificant activities while setting aside important tasks. Usually, these insignificant tasks are much more enjoyable to do than the important tasks at hand.

Procrastination leads to multiple problems in the world of business as far as productivity goes. For example, playing videogames when you should be working on a project often leads to substandard output, missed deadlines, and stress. This occurs especially if you wait too long before finally deciding to finish an objective.

Business Habit #3: Looking For Challenges

A reliable way of reducing procrastination is to invest more in productivity. It just makes sense for you to keep yourself busy in order to avoid wasting time. First, take a look at another Business Habit that can bring you more productivity – *looking for challenges.*

When running a business or working on your career, you may grow to despise challenges. They tend to be stressful, annoying, and even an indication of possible failure. When viewed with such negativity, you tend to generally avoid all forms of challenges in your life.

However, do you think this attitude toward challenges will bring you success in the future? Of course not! In fact, no successful business ever came to be without countless challenges that their leaders have overcome.

Instead of perceiving challenges negatively, take them as opportunities to grow and stay productive.

What better way to reduce procrastination than to find more opportunities to become productive?

Remember in the world of business, it your duty to stay competitive. A Business Habit that can help you do this is to actively seek improvements by constantly *challenging yourself*.

There are many ways for you to find these challenges for yourself and your business. One is to *observe* your competition and figure out their edges against you. Once you acquire this information, challenge yourself to do something in response to your competition. Is their product more appealing for a certain demographic? Are they making more money than you simply due to pricing issues? These are the simple questions that can help you find challenges.

Dealing with Procrastination

While creating opportunities for you to be productive is a reliable way of preventing procrastination, it may not be enough eliminate it altogether. In fact, you probably will not be able to completely remove procrastination from your life forever.

Fighting procrastination and keeping up with your productivity is a lifelong journey. You have to constantly make an effort to focus on completing relevant tasks and fulfilling responsibilities, while doing *just enough* for yourself to slow down and enjoy.

In other words, aiming to directly eliminate procrastination by removing all unimportant activities in your schedule will never be effective for sustaining productivity.

Instead, focus on finding *progress* with everything that you do – in relation to your business goals and objectives. This simple mindset is the key for dealing with procrastination most effectively.

An excellent way to demonstrate this mindset is by following the principle of the *Ultradian Rhythm.*

Business Habit #4: Taking 30-Minute Breaks

In the discovery of researcher *Nathan Kleitman,* he described the human body's tendency to undergo a 90-minute cycle at night. In this cycle, the human brain goes through five stages of sleep, switching from light to heavy brain activity. He called this concept the *Basic Rest-Activity Cycle.*

Kleitman also found out that the human brain operates in this cycle during the day, following a rhythm of 90 minutes every time. Thus, the *Ultradian Rhythm* was coined.

The Ultradian Rhythm describes the activity of the brain sending out certain signals after a 90-minute session of work. These signals include hunger, inattentiveness, and sleepiness. In other words, your brain is telling you to stop and recharge.

However, most people tend to ignore these signals and carry on even after 90 minutes of intense work. With modern lifestyle, people tend to use caffeine and other snacks to suppress the Ultradian Rhythm. Although you will have the ability to continue working past the 90-minute mark, you can definitely observe the decline in performance.

With this being said, it is a good habit to take 30-minute breaks after 90-minutes of hard work. These 30-minute breaks are enough for your mind to continue performing in peak condition. Also take note that these breaks must consist of complete relaxation and rehydration. Take these opportunities to perform stretching exercises, drink a glass of water, close your eyes, and just breathe.

You should also allow everyone working under you to practice this resting habit. By now, you should know their productivity is your productivity as well. Understand that your subordinates also need rest and a healthy mind for maximum output.

Other ways of Dealing with Procrastination

Procrastination is a lasting threat to your business and the individual productivity of your team. It can even be a threat to your family and your social life, but when it comes to your business/career, you should take the issue of procrastination seriously.

First of all, realize you are not the only one who can procrastinate in your business. Also, consider the fact that the procrastination of other members in your business will affect you as well. In other words, the productivity of every single person in your team is imperative for success.

In order to deal with the problem of procrastination in your business, observe the following strategies:

1. **Search and Destroy (Procrastination Triggers)** – Every person has something in his life that he considers the *guilty pleasure* when it comes to procrastination. It is something close to an addiction that never fails to cause a person to procrastinate whenever the opportunity rears its ugly head. In your place of business, it is important for you to spot these triggers as early as possible and eliminate its source. These triggers are commonly found in:

    a. *Social Media Networking Sites* – Who does not log on to social media websites frequently these days? One of the most prevalent problems in most offices today is the presence of an *epidemic* in the disguise of *Facebook, Twitter, Instagram, Pinterest, Google+, etc.* While it may not be a crime to check your friend's baby photos, your best friend's engagement announcement, or your mother's progress in an online game, it definitely hurts the productivity in a place meant for business. Employ strict rules in your place of business against the use of social media during working hours. Unless, of course, you have a social media team who promotes your business online.

b. *Smartphone Apps* – Another problem caused by modern technology is the introduction of games and other apps that can distract anyone from productivity. If you are running a business, it can be quite a problem since your staff can easily hide them whenever you check. You cannot prevent them from accessing their phones during work hours either. The most efficient way to lessen procrastination brought about by smartphone apps is to give your team a sense of responsibility through motivation. There are ideas on how to do this later on in this book.

c. *Lazy Staff* – As a business, you should know that one person can bring the entire place down. An inefficient member who causes distractions in your place of work is not exactly common, but these people can appear when you least expect them to. If you are running a business, make sure everyone contributes to the accomplishment of your business objectives.

2. **Clutter** – Old magazines, empty coffee cups, notes, and other forms of clutter do more than just make the place untidy. They also distract you from doing more important tasks or bother you enough to prevent you from working efficiently. In your place of work, establish strict rules to put away clutter before it even accumulates.

3. **Improve Discipline** – Every person has varying levels of self-discipline, but when it comes to productivity and business, everyone is required to have strong self-discipline, which is integral for success. As an individual, you should also make sure you have the willpower needed to complete each objective, no matter how difficult things get.

When following these strategies for preventing procrastination, make sure you set an example by using these strategies on yourself. Remember that if you are running a business, *your* own effort as its leader is most important. This also nurtures mutual respect amongst the members of your business.

Rewarding a Job Well Done

Every person in this world has limits. No matter how professional you think you are or how motivated you have become in accomplishing your goal, you will still feel strong urges to procrastinate every once in a while. As stated earlier, fighting procrastination and maintaining productivity is a lifelong process. You never actually reach a point where you will never be at risk for procrastination. Instead, you need to maintain a mindset that will always *choose* to be more productive.

This involves staying on track with your goals, always answering for your responsibilities, and keeping yourself motivated every single day. All these can be accomplished by doing the simple act of *rewarding* others and yourself for a job well done.

There are two known forms of rewards in the world of business management – *extrinsic* rewards and *intrinsic* rewards.

Extrinsic rewards are basically tangible rewards given to deserving members. This usually comes in the form of cash, raises and other benefits. Of course, it is a very effective motivational tool for managers.

You can use any other tangible item to reward someone's hard work, but surprisingly enough, it may never be as efficient as intrinsic rewards when it comes to motivating your team.

Unless if you are a manufacturer managing factory workers, the output of your team members are mostly from their own effort, intelligence, experience, and creativity. This is why their own engagement with your business and their motivation to engage is equally as important as getting the job done itself.

There are four ways to describe intrinsic rewards:

1. **Progress** – The first, very important, intrinsic reward is the sense of *being significant* in a team. This means you feel the sense of progress with your contributions. This takes into account the impact of what a member has done to accomplish a particular goal/objective of the organization.

2. **Meaningfulness** – Another important intrinsic reward is the sense of *accomplishment* for every ounce of effort given. Remember that this refers to the personal sense of accomplishment of a member, and not the organization/business as a whole. Is he happy with his work? Does he feel fulfilled after successfully completing his tasks?

3. **Competence** – The sense of proficiency is priceless, especially after giving it the best of

your ability to finish a given task. This goes hand in hand with the senses of accomplishment and significance – being able to see real progress from all your efforts.

4. **Choice** – Lastly, it is important for any person to feel always *in charge* when dealing with responsibilities. This is much more to motivating than just following orders directly to the letter. Trusting in another member's judgment in accomplishing an objective is also a strong characteristic as a leader.

In other words, intrinsic rewards are *self-imposed* rewards. If you are running a business, the only thing you can do is to express your support as a leader and trust in the individual skills of your team members.

Chapter Activity:

This chapter's activity is a little more straightforward. You need to gather every person involved with your business or organization, and call a general meeting. For this, you will need to have an established timetable and a checklist of objectives for the current month. You may also want to have a notepad ready to write down important details.

This time, you will talk as *equals* and not as a boss talking to subordinates. Begin the meeting by discussing your monthly objectives and checking on the progress of each team member. After making sure that everybody is doing their job, proceed by sharing your long-term goals (see Chapter 1) for the business.

Observe your team's reaction. Do they believe in your vision? Can they picture the business being at the point described in your visualizations? This is the part where you take direct input from every member as if they own the company with you.

Here are some things you can do during this meeting:

1. *Ask for feedback regarding your long-term goals.*

2. *Listen to every idea and suggestions that may improve the business.*

3. *Accept constructive criticisms and take them as opportunities for growth.*

4. *Talk about future objectives and consider adjustments.*

5. *Ask for opinions and suggestions regarding your timetable.*

Remember to thank every person who attended the meeting, and show your sincere appreciation for their cooperation. After the meeting, you are almost guaranteed to receive more output from your team and better results for your business.

Chapter 4 – Organization & Prioritization

By the end of this Chapter, you will have learned all about:

- *How organization in your place of business is relevant for success*

- *Why prioritization is always more valuable than multitasking*

- *Simple workplace organization tips for better productivity*

In anyone's business and professional life, disorganization is the equivalent of stress, poor performance, and failure. The relationship between organization and success is simple, yet very powerful. It affects every person's work performance, as well as the entire organization itself.

Still, it is easy to overlook organization as a major contributor to success, especially with everything going on all around your business. The next thing you know, *everything* is in chaos.

As a business leader, it is important for you to ensure that the collective effort of your team moves you closer to achieving your business objectives.

Business Habit #5: Clearing Desks

A simple aspect of staying productive as an individual is keeping your work desk clean and functional. Cluttering vital sections of the workplace can lead to the stressful sight of stacked papers, missing tools, and a variety of other problems.

As the leader, you need to employ preventive measures to avoid deterring the productivity of your team due to messiness. Establish strict rules in your place of business about the cleanliness of desks before, during, and after work hours.

Prioritize or Multitask?

Multitasking can give any person the illusion of accomplishing more when, in fact, it can be a very inefficient way to work. Multitasking literally divides your focus onto two or more tasks, causing you to perform poorly in all of them, while stressing yourself out even more.

Never mistake multitasking for increased productivity. Instead, you should encourage your team to start focusing on one task at a time. This makes sure a particular task receives undivided attention, which ensures high quality output.

Prioritizing Objectives

Also make sure your list of daily objectives is duly organized depending on urgency. In order to maximize productivity, you need to prioritize the *most important* and *grueling* task.

Practice working with your people and encourage teamwork to complete the most important task of the day. Bear in mind that no objective is too great for a determined group of people working well together.

Choosing a task

In the real world, the most difficult tasks usually are more relevant than the rest, and these tasks deserve to be executed with your team's full capabilities, since they usually offer the most rewards. Remember that it is also a tendency for the body to decline when it comes to work performance as the hours go by. By choosing to work on the smaller objectives first, the body may run out of energy before relevant progress even begins. With this being said, guide your team and help them prioritize tasks for maximum efficiency.

Choosing the Right People

A business is like a chain. It is only as strong as the *weakest link.* Every single person in your business should contribute to a common goal. Keep in mind that sometimes the mistake of one person may render the efforts of others useless.

Managing your team should start from the *hiring* process

It is a known fact that the best people create the best companies. The bulk of the success of your business will come from the people you hire. You should also monitor the performance of each person as time goes by. Accept nothing but the best from your team, and you will receive the best in return.

Chapter 5 – Managing Your Team: Bonus Habits

Business Habits For Increased Productivity And Sustained Success

By the end of this Chapter, you will have learned all about:

- *Additional 'Business Habits' for sustained success*

Congratulations for reaching the final chapter of this book. This final chapter contains additional Business Habits that will help you sustain your productivity and success in the long run.

Business Habit #6: Give them Space

As a business leader, you may feel the need to be involved with everybody's work. To a certain degree, this is effective in supervising the individual work of each member. However, you should not irritate your subordinates by criticizing and commenting on every small action. Let them work and trust in their judgment – why else would you hire them in the first place?

You can also schedule frequent meetings with certain people to stay updated with relevant matters. Also try to make these meetings short, as to not waste too much of the other person's time.

Business Habit #7: Rehydrate your Team

Never forget that everybody depends on hydration to function. While everybody should already be familiar with the old rule of drinking eight to ten glasses of water every day, not everybody actually does it.

Headaches, heat, eyestrain, and a lot of other symptoms common in the office can easily be avoided by proper hydration. See to it that you provide a steady supply of drinking water in your business for your team. Also, encourage them to rehydrate whenever they take breaks.

Business Habit #8: Adjust

An important aspect of creating a timetable and keeping a checklist of daily objectives is checking to see if the system you have created works perfectly. Do not settle for 'okay' results, and always seek improvements.

Take a look at your timetable and the things you've accomplished so far with it. Be creative, and always find ways to improve the productivity of your team. Also, provide your own input to help your team adjust for better results.

Business Habit #9: Practice Effective Delegation

Mediocre results often arise from delegating a task to the wrong person. This is why you should know every member of your team personally. Consider their strengths and weaknesses while continually evaluating their performance on certain tasks.

However, you should also give everyone a fair chance. Encourage the growth of every person in your team by giving them responsibilities you think they are capable of. You can also assign someone more experienced to mentor this person and improve their skills as well as their ability to work as a team.

Just make sure you leverage the skills of your most trusted people on extremely important tasks. The key is to rely on the strength on one person, and believe in the potential of another.

Business Habit #10: Inform Them

The ignorance of one person can have dire effects on a team. By making sure the information in your business is synchronized between each person, you are effectively preventing the occurrence of errors and misunderstandings.

Make it a habit to report results – big and small – accurately and as soon as they become available. Respect the right of your team to know everything they need about the entire organization. This will also make them feel more involved with the business, which is a relevant factor in keeping them motivated.

Ultimately, you will need to believe in the vision you have created as a team. Once you figure out the way to share the same vision with every person in your business, no obstacle will slow you down ever again.

Conclusion

Thank you again for purchasing this book!

I hope this book was able to help you increase your productivity and maximize the success of your business.

Business Habits For Increased Productivity And Sustained Success

The next step is to continue writing in your personal journal, updating your timetable, and completing every single task in your checklist of daily objectives.

Trust in everyone, but depend on yourself as the leader.

Remember that success, just like productivity, is an ongoing experience. You have to fight for it every single day, and prove that you deserve it more than anything.

Thank you and good luck!

www.ingramcontent.com/pod-product-compliance
Lightning Source LLC
Chambersburg PA
CBHW070714180526
45167CB00004B/1475